Discovering

CRICKETS AND GRASSHOPPERS

Keith Porter

Illustrations by Wendy Meadway

The Bookwright Press
New York · 1986

Discovering Nature

Discovering Ants
Discovering Bees and Wasps
Discovering Beetles
Discovering Birds of Prey
Discovering Butterflies and Moths
Discovering Flies
Discovering Frogs and Toads

Discovering Crickets and Grasshoppers
Discovering Rabbits and Hares
Discovering Snakes and Lizards
Discovering Spiders
Discovering Squirrels
Discovering Worms

Further titles are in preparation

All photographs from Oxford Scientific Films

First published in the
United States in 1986 by
The Bookwright Press
387 Park Avenue South
New York, NY 10016

First published in 1986 by
Wayland (Publishers) Limited
61 Western Road, Hove
East Sussex, BN3 1JD, England

© Copyright 1986 Wayland (Publishers) Limited

ISBN 0-531-18096-4
Library of Congress Catalog Card Number: 86-70990

Typeset by Alphabet Typesetters Limited
Printed in Italy by Sagdos S.p.A., Milan

Cover *A grasshopper warms up in the sun in Arizona.*
Frontispiece *A bush cricket, or katydid, from Trinidad.*

Contents

1
Introducing Crickets and Grasshoppers

The meadow grasshopper lives in fields and meadows.

Crickets and Grasshoppers as Insects

Crickets and grasshoppers are found all over the world. By looking at their shapes we can tell that they are insects. Their bodies are divided into three main parts: the head is the smallest part and is found at the front end. The middle part is called the **thorax**, and it holds the three pairs of legs and two pairs of wings. The largest section is called the **abdomen**. This is often hidden under the wings.

As in all insects, the bodies of crickets and grasshoppers are made of a hard, light material called **chitin** (kite-in). This forms a tough "skin" or "shell," which acts like a skeleton and gives the insect its shape. Insects do not have bones inside their bodies as we do.

Insects can be divided into about thirty groups. The crickets and grasshoppers make up one of the oldest groups called the *Orthoptera*, which means "straight-winged." Today, there are over 17,000 types of crickets and grasshoppers in the world. Almost all of them live in warm, sunny countries.

Crickets and grasshoppers are among the noisiest insects. Many sing loud, chirpy songs from the safety of a grassy hillside or bush. They are also among the best jumpers in the animal world.

People have always had a special affection for crickets. Some have been made famous in literature, including the house cricket in Charles Dickens' *Cricket on the Hearth*, and the talking cricket in the story of Pinocchio.

Most crickets are noisy insects but the oak bush cricket makes very little sound. It lives in cold countries, eats plants and sleeps through the winter.

The Body Shapes of Crickets and Grasshoppers

Crickets and grasshoppers have long, narrow bodies. All have rounded heads and squarish thoraxes. The head holds the eyes, a pair of "feelers," or **antennae**, and a large mouth. Every cricket and grasshopper has a pair of large eyes on its head. These are called **compound eyes**, because they are made up of many tiny parts, each of which sees only a fraction of the overall picture. Like most insects, crickets and grasshoppers are good at seeing moving things, but poor at seeing details. Their compound eyes can also see colors, just like our eyes. Many crickets and grasshoppers have two or three tiny, **simple eyes** on top

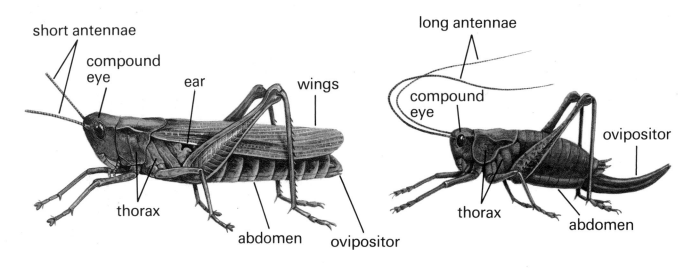

GRASSHOPPER

BUSH CRICKET

of the head too. These cannot see a "picture," but can tell night from day.

The thorax is covered by a large plate, or shield, which is called a pronotum. This acts like armor in protecting the top of the thorax. It also covers the back of the head and base of the wings.

All crickets and grasshoppers have two pairs of short legs and one pair of huge, back legs. Most grasshoppers, and some kinds of crickets, have two pairs of long wings. The straight, leathery pair of front wings usually covers the finer, more delicate back pair. The hind wings are much bigger than the front, and are kept folded when not being used to fly. Other crickets and grasshoppers have very short wings.

The abdomen of every cricket and grasshopper is made up of ten rings, or segments, of hard armor. These segments help the insect to bend its

This grasshopper has much longer back legs than most other grasshoppers.

abdomen while still protecting the inside of the body. The abdomen contains the gut and special parts that make eggs and **sperm cells**.

Different Kinds of Crickets and Grasshoppers

There are two main kinds of insects within the *Orthoptera* group. One kind makes up a group we call the crickets; the others we call grasshoppers. Crickets are different from grasshoppers in several ways.

The cricket group includes true crickets, bush crickets, camel crickets, and mole crickets. Bush crickets differ from true crickets and mole crickets in that their ears are situated on their front legs instead of on the sides of the abdomen. The bush crickets are sometimes called long-horned grasshoppers or katydids. Crickets usually have long antennae, often longer than their bodies, and short wings. Some kinds have such short

Like most crickets, the speckled bush cricket has very long antennae.

wings that they cannot fly. The female cricket has a long, pointed "sword" sticking out from the end of her abdomen. This is called an **ovipositor** and is used to squeeze eggs into cracks and crevices.

The grasshopper group includes all familiar grasshoppers and a few kinds of large grasshoppers, we call locusts. There are about 10,000 kinds of insects

in the grasshopper group. Unlike crickets, grasshoppers usually have long wings, which cover most of the body. Their antennae are always shorter than the body. Female grasshoppers do not have such large ovipositors as crickets; theirs are small and often difficult to see.

Crickets hide away during the day and become active as night approaches. Grasshoppers are active

One of the biggest grasshoppers is the giant grasshopper from Central America.

during the day and spend much of their time sitting in the hot sunshine. Crickets and grasshoppers live in many places. Bush crickets live in bushes or trees, while true crickets live on the ground or in burrows in the soil. Most grasshoppers live in grassy places, but a few kinds live in hot, dry deserts.

2
Jumpers and Singers

Grasshoppers and crickets have long, strong back legs.

Jumping and Flying

Crickets and grasshoppers are well known as leaping insects. Their first two pairs of legs are used only for walking. Their huge back legs have fat "thighs," which contain the muscles needed to push the whole insect through the air in one leap. Many can jump several times their own length, but they are also so small and light that they do not hurt themselves when they land.

Many grasshoppers and crickets move mainly by leaping. For various crickets, leaping is their only way of escaping enemies. Their short wings are useless for flying. Most crickets and grasshoppers leap in a straight line and are easy to follow.

Some grasshoppers and crickets can increase the distance they leap by using their wings. They use short, whirring flights to extend the leap into a sort of glide. This glide-leap can trace a winding path, which confuses enemies and is difficult to follow.

Some grasshoppers, including locusts, use their wings to fly long distances. They are often helped by winds or by warm, rising air currents. Both the front and back pairs of wings are flapped and this helps to lift the insect off the ground and push it

Above *A desert locust in flight.*

through the air. The muscles that power the wings are packed tightly into the thorax.

Many crickets cannot fly because their wings are far too short. Those that can fly include the bush crickets and some mole crickets. The mole crickets flap their short wings much faster than grasshoppers do, and as a result have a slow "buzzing" flight.

This diagram shows how grasshoppers and crickets use their back legs for leaping.

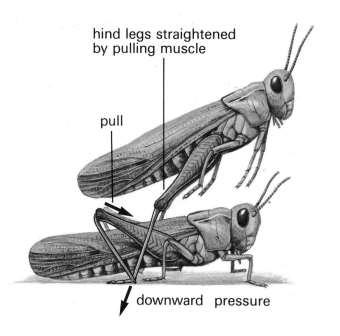

hind legs straightened by pulling muscle

pull

downward pressure

How Grasshoppers Talk to Each Other

Grasshoppers are famous for their buzzing or chirpy songs. These sounds are their way of talking to one another. Sometimes both male and female grasshoppers can make sounds. However, the males are always the best, and loudest, singers. They are responsible for most of the chirping we hear in the countryside. Some young grasshoppers can make sounds too, but their songs are quiet and rarely heard.

Male grasshoppers sing songs to warn off other males and to attract females for **mating**. The female's song is mainly used in courtship as an "answer" to the male's song.

Grasshoppers produce sounds by rubbing the insides of their back legs over hard ridges, or veins, on their front wings. This is called **stridulating**. The inside of each back

Grasshoppers communicate with sounds made by rubbing the insides of their back legs over hard ridges on their front wings.

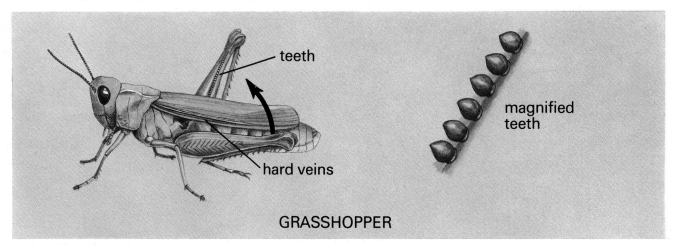

teeth

hard veins

magnified teeth

GRASSHOPPER

different song. Some make long, buzzing noises while others use short, ticking sounds, rather like morse code.

Sounds are no use to a grasshopper unless another grasshopper can hear them. Every grasshopper has one ear on each side of the body. These ears are rather like tiny "drums" set inside a hollow on the first segment of the abdomen. Each eardrum works like a tiny microphone, picking up sounds and passing them, as messages, along nerves to the brain.

Below *A close-up of a grasshopper's ear.*

A European grasshopper stridulating or "singing."

leg has a row of tiny teeth, rather like a comb. When this row of teeth is rubbed against the wing it produces a noise. You can make a similar noise by rubbing your nail along a comb.

Each type of grasshopper has a

Songs at Dusk

Crickets are among the noisiest of all insects. Their loud chirps are heard during the night or early evening. In the tropics, they fill the nights with sound. Their chirps are much higher and more piercing than those of grasshoppers.

Only male true crickets can produce sounds, while a few female bush crickets can also produce a much quieter sound. Some young crickets can also produce a chirping sound.

Cricket sounds are made in a very different way from those of grasshoppers. The wings of a cricket overlap each other at the base, and can be rubbed quickly together. One wing has a hard, ridged vein, which we call a file. The other wing has a hard ridge, which is called a scraper. By quickly rubbing the scraper across the file a sound is made.

True crickets have the scraper on the

By quickly rubbing its wings together, a male cricket can make loud, chirpy noises.

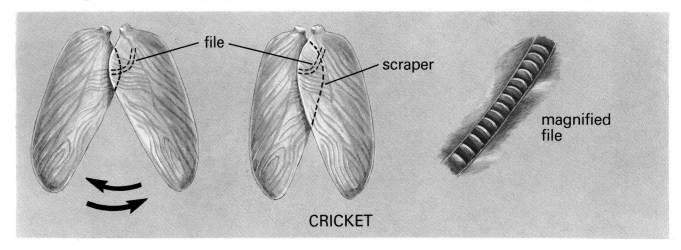

file

scraper

magnified file

CRICKET

left, front wing, while bush crickets have the scraper on the right wing. Every type of cricket has a different song, each being recognized by others of the same type.

A North American field cricket sings to attract a female.

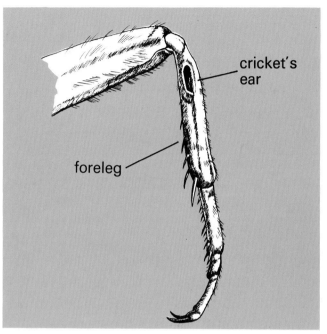

Unlike grasshoppers, crickets' ears are on their front legs.

A cricket's ears are on its front legs! A swollen part, near the "knee," holds a tiny "drum skin" inside a hollow. These ears work in the same way as those of a grasshopper and help the cricket to tell the direction and distance of another singing cricket.

Warming up for Action

Like all insects, crickets and grasshoppers are cold-blooded animals. This means that they cannot keep their own bodies warm unless the surroundings are warm. They heat up by moving into warm places, or by basking in the sun. Humans, cats, dogs, and other mammals are warm-blooded. They are able to keep their bodies at a steady temperature wherever they are.

Crickets and grasshoppers can only move quickly, or sing, if their bodies are warm enough. That is why most live in warm parts of the world. Many types spend much of the day sitting in the sun to warm up.

Many crickets and grasshoppers are dark colored, to help them warm up quickly. Dark colors are better at soaking up the warmth of the sun than pale colors. On a sunny day, a dark car tire can become too hot to touch, while a white painted fence stays quite cool.

Even in deserts there are

A desert grasshopper basks in the sun.

grasshoppers and crickets that bask in the sun. They do this in the early morning to warm up quickly, so they can leap about and feed. By mid-morning they begin to avoid the hot sun and seek the shade, often crawling under rocks to hide. As the desert cools down, the crickets and grasshoppers once again come out to sunbathe and keep warm.

Many grasshoppers are found

The Namib desert cricket has long legs, which help to lift it off the hot sand.

basking on bare patches of earth, among grasses and plants. Here they can press their bodies onto the hot soil and soak up warmth from the ground. Their dark color patterns also help to disguise them on these bare patches. Indeed, some are very difficult to see until they twitch a leg or an antenna.

3
Food and Feeding

Some grasshoppers, such as this long-horned grasshopper, eat the pollen in flowers.

Plant-eaters and Meat-eaters

The mouth of a grasshopper or cricket is made up of many parts. The front of the mouth is covered by a hard "upper lip," which can be moved upward to let food into the mouth. Inside the mouth are two pairs of jaws. The first pair are called **mandibles**, and have sharp, jagged edges which can cut up and grind food. Behind them is a smaller pair of jaws, called **maxillae**, which have a few small teeth at their edges. They are used to guide food into the mouth and help to chop it up.

The maxillae each hold a pair of long finger-like "feelers," which are called **palps**. These palps are like tiny tongues and are used to taste food before biting. The back of the mouth is shut by a hard "lower lip," which also has a pair of palps. This lip helps to keep food from falling out of the mouth.

Most grasshoppers and bush crickets eat grasses, leaves, or plant stems. This food is chopped into small pieces by the scissor-like movements of the mandibles, and then swallowed. Some grasshoppers can eat huge amounts of grass and they can be pests in fields of crops.

Many crickets, including some bush crickets, have very powerful jaws. They eat both plants and small animals. Some crickets eat the dead bodies of insects and spiders, while others catch and eat live insects and worms. Most feed at night when they must "feel" for food rather than see it.

An oak bush cricket eating a dead fly.

Plagues of Locusts

Most grasshoppers live alone and come together only to mate. Locusts are unusual in that they have young that sometimes stay together after hatching. Young locusts are called **hoppers**. They often stay together and move in groups, called bands, in search of food. If bands of hoppers join up, they can soon become pests, eating every green plant in their path. These hoppers eventually grow into fully-winged adult locusts, which also form into huge swarms. Some swarms can contain millions of locusts, and may cover over 100 sq km (39 sq miles) of land. These plagues of locusts often eat enormous quantities of crops, and this can lead to food shortages and people starving.

Such huge swarms happen only once every few years, often after hoppers have been forced to move

These desert locust hoppers have undergone five skin changes.

together by floods or a shortage of food. For much of the time, locusts live quite happily as solitary insects.

Some kinds of locusts have two different forms. One form lives alone and has hoppers and adults that are colored to match their background. The other form lives crowded together; they are colored black and yellow. It is this "crowded" form of locust that makes up the destructive swarms of adults and bands of hoppers.

Despite their numbers and fame, there are only ten or so kinds of grasshoppers that can be called locusts. Some, such as the desert and red locust, live in Africa; others live in South America, the Mediterranean and Australia. One kind, called the

A hopper, or young desert locust, after its third skin change. It will molt two more times before becoming an adult.

migratory locust, is found in many parts of the world and can fly for long distances.

4
The Life History of Crickets and Grasshoppers

A pair of short-horned grasshoppers mating. The smaller of the two is the male.

From Egg to Adult

All insects go through different stages of life. Crickets and grasshoppers have three stages. They begin life as eggs, each of which hatches into a **larva**, or **nymph**. The nymphs finally grow into adults.

After mating with a male, the female cricket or grasshopper lays her eggs. Grasshopper and cricket eggs are often shaped like tiny, white bananas. Like all insect eggs, they have tough outside shells, which are made from chitin. The shell protects the egg from being squashed. Most types of eggs are coated in a kind of "varnish," which keeps the egg from drying out.

The eggs of grasshoppers and crickets often take months to hatch. Some types produce eggs that last through the winter, while the eggs of others can survive hot, dry summers.

The first stage hatches from a

cricket or grasshopper egg as a strange looking creature called a **pronymph**. It has no legs or antennae and moves by wriggling. Minutes after hatching, the skin of this creature breaks open, and a tiny grasshopper or cricket nymph crawls into the world.

All grasshopper and cricket nymphs look much like their parents. The main difference is that nymphs have tiny bumps where the wings should be. These are called wing-pads. The nymphs eat the same food as the adults, and grow by shedding the old skin and growing a new, larger skin. A

A grasshopper nymph looks almost like its parents but it has not yet developed wings.

nymph sheds its skin four to ten times (depending upon the type of grasshopper or cricket it is) before becoming an adult. At each skin change, its wing-pads get bigger.

Unlike many other insects, grasshoppers and crickets do not have a **pupa** stage. The change from nymph to adult is simply a skin change. Once adult, they do not grow any larger and never shed their skin again.

The Life History of the Grasshopper

Most grasshoppers lay their eggs in the ground. The female uses the tip of her abdomen to dig a hole in sand or soil. Some kinds can dig as deep as 16 cm (6 in). As she digs, the female swallows air until her abdomen blows up like a balloon. This helps her to force her body down into soft soil.

In this hole the female lays from three to 200 eggs, depending upon the type of grasshopper she is. The eggs are laid in a kind of froth, which hardens into a spongy mass. The froth protects the eggs from drying out. The mass of eggs and froth is called an egg pod.

Each female will produce several egg pods during her few months of life. The eggs will stay in the ground for up to six months and hatch when the weather becomes warmer, or when the rainy season arrives. The pronymphs hatch together, and force a path through the froth and soil. At the soil surface they split open after a few minutes and tiny grasshoppers leap out.

Most grasshopper nymphs will feed for a few months on plants. They grow in stages, by changing their skins, and after five or so changes become full sized adults. Only then can males and females mate and begin the cycle all over again. Grasshoppers that live in

A female desert locust pushes her ovipositor into the sand to lay her eggs.

tropical countries may grow from egg to adult in two or three months. Others need a full year.

A desert locust nymph, or hopper, after its first skin change.

After twenty-one days the eggs hatch. The pronymphs push their way up to the surface of the sand and each one splits to reveal a tiny grasshopper called a nymph.

A pair of crickets mating at night in a forest in Malaysia. After mating the female lays her eggs.

The Life History of the Cricket

Crickets lay their eggs in the ground, in rotten wood, or in plant stems. Most true crickets have long, straight ovipositors, which look like needles. They use the ovipositor to lay eggs one at a time in the ground. Bush crickets, or katydids, have long, curved ovipositors, often longer than the rest of the body. These crickets use their ovipositors to lay eggs inside plant stems or sometimes in the ground.

Cricket eggs are usually laid singly or in small clusters, and are not usually surrounded by a frothy pod. The eggs remain in the ground, or in plants, for several months, often passing over cold winters or dry summers.

The tiny pronymphs of some crickets have a special "egg-burster" on the head. This is used to force a way out of the egg and into the open air. The first stage of a cricket nymph is a

A speckled bush cricket nymph. At this stage in its life it has no wings.

tiny copy of the adult, except that it has no wings, and the female does have an ovipositor.

Crickets feed mainly on plants, but they also eat small animals. At first, the nymphs can feed only on plants, as their jaws are weak and small. Most bush cricket nymphs go through five or six skin changes. True crickets can have ten or more skin changes, and in some the nymph may **hibernate** in an underground burrow.

Many crickets take a full year to grow from egg to adult. In warm countries some need only six months. In cooler countries, some true crickets take two years to reach the adult stage.

5
Enemies and Survival

Many insects are eaten by spiders. This hunting spider has caught a large, long-horned grasshopper.

Enemies of Crickets and Grasshoppers

Crickets and grasshoppers have many enemies at all stages in the life cycle. Very few eggs will ever hatch to grow and become adults, because most will be eaten by other animals.

You might expect the eggs of crickets and grasshoppers to be well protected, since most are buried in the soil. But many eggs are attacked by the larvae of certain kinds of flies. These flies, which are **parasites**, lay their eggs on the eggs of crickets and grasshoppers. The fly larvae then hatch out and eat the eggs of the cricket or grasshopper.

The young nymphs of crickets and grasshoppers make tasty meals for other insects and small animals. Many are caught and eaten by beetles, spiders, mice, lizards and small birds. Some nymphs avoid these enemies by hiding away among leaves on the ground or in bushes.

Adult grasshoppers and crickets fall prey to larger animals. Many birds will spend most of their time searching for insects. Some, such as egrets, follow herds of large animals and catch grasshoppers that are disturbed by the feeding cattle or even by elephants.

Large swarms of locusts attract many birds and other animals. Herons, storks, crows, and kites, will gather to feast on them. Rats, cats, mongooses, and jackals will also eat locusts and bush crickets. In some parts of the world even humans join in the feast.

Adult grasshoppers and crickets are sometimes eaten from the inside by parasites, which include the larvae of certain flies, and many types of worms and **funguses**.

A gecko eating a locust in Sudan. Many other animals like to eat locusts.

Hiding from Enemies

Most crickets and grasshoppers are brown or green in color. These colors match their surroundings and so help to **camouflage** these insects from their enemies.

Grasshoppers that live on the ground are usually patterned with brown or gray. These patterns blend into the background, making the grasshoppers difficult to see against dead leaves or on bare, stony ground. Many true crickets and grouse locusts (also called ground hoppers) are patterned in a similar way. They may also have strange, spiky shapes which help to disguise them even further.

Bush crickets and grasshoppers that live among grasses, often have striped patterns of green, brown, or purple. These colors match some of the colors found on the grasses among which they live. The stripes run along the body and seem to line up with the grass stems on which the insects sit. Some crickets and grasshoppers have extremely long bodies and pointed heads, which also help to conceal their shape.

Bush crickets, which live in trees and bushes, are either brown or green. Their wings exactly match the shape and patterns of leaves and often have marks that look like the scars and spots found on real leaves. Some types of bush crickets are very spiky and

By looking like a leaf this katydid, or bush cricket is well camouflaged.

look more like thorny branches than insects.

One type of grasshopper or cricket may develop several different color patterns. There can be up to twenty different varieties of one insect. Each pattern matches a certain type of

The stick-like shape of this grasshopper helps it to hide in plants and bushes and therefore avoid being eaten.

background and ensures that, because of their camouflage, some adults at least will escape their enemies.

Frightening Enemies with Color and Shape

Crickets and grasshoppers have several ways of frightening off their enemies. Some have bright colors, which warn that they are poisonous or taste bad. Some of these grasshoppers protect themselves by producing a poisonous froth from parts of the body. The poisons are often obtained from the plants that the grasshopper eats.

The most common way to startle enemies is to confuse them with bright

The black, yellow and red colors of the elegant grasshopper warn predators that it is poisonous.

colors. Many types of grasshoppers have brightly colored hind wings or abdomens. The band-winged grasshoppers have blue, yellow, or red hind wings, marked with a bold black band. When they are resting, they rely for safety upon the camouflaged pattern of their outer bodies and front wings. But if they are disturbed, or attacked, they can quickly open their wings and fly off in a brilliant flash of color. When they land on the ground, this bright color is quickly hidden once more, so they seem to have disappeared. This trick usually fools birds and lizards that attack grasshoppers.

The Australian mountain grasshopper has a similar habit. It has a bright blue, black, and red abdomen, which it shows off by flicking forward its wings. This shock display of bright colors often scares away attackers. A few grasshoppers and crickets have nymphs that look like ants. This protects them from birds who have learned that ants can sting or bite. As a last resort, many grasshoppers and crickets can shed a leg if necessary, to escape from harm. Many adults have only one hind leg by the time they reach old age.

The Australian mountain grasshopper scares enemies by flashing its bright abdomen.

6
Some Unusual Crickets and Grasshoppers

A ground hopper is so-called because it cannot fly.

Grouse Locusts and Camel Crickets

Some insects in the grasshopper and cricket group do not look like ordinary crickets or grasshoppers. They include grouse locusts, camel crickets, and mole crickets.

The grouse, or pygmy locusts are small relatives of the grasshoppers. Over 1,000 types live around the world but most are found in hot countries. They are sometimes called ground hoppers because many cannot fly. They are easily recognized by the pointed, backward extention of the thorax that covers the wings and much of the abdomen. Grouse locusts often live in marshes or swamps and eat mosses or other small plants. Many of them are well camouflaged and can swim in pools or streams.

The camel crickets and New Zealand wetas belong to a group of crickets that often live in caves. The

The cave cricket from Malaysia looks nothing like other crickets.

This grouse locust is well camouflaged for living in the desert.

North American cave, or camel cricket, is a wingless, humpbacked cricket that lives under stones or in caves during the day. It comes out at night to hunt for small, and often dead, insects and is unusual because it cannot sing, and has no ears.

Camel crickets have been taken to many parts of the world by chance. They are often carried in the soil of plants to greenhouses and gardens in other countries.

Mole Crickets and Field Crickets

Mole crickets and field crickets spend much of their life underground. Adult field crickets live in burrows, as do some of the older nymphs. It is only the young nymphs that live above the ground, feeding on plants. The older nymphs use their back legs to dig into the ground. As they dig, they use their back legs to kick soil out of the hole.

Some field crickets live in colonies, which may cover an area of several square meters. Each adult has its own burrow and often sings, during the daytime, from the entrance. Adult male field crickets shape their burrows into funnels. They use the entrance to the burrow like a trumpet to "throw" their chirpy songs out into the air for up to 20 m (65 ft) or so. Their long distance singing attracts females to their

Field crickets live in underground burrows.

burrows. Some types of field crickets alter the shape of their burrows to produce different musical notes.

Mole crickets have large, spade-like front legs and broad, flat thoraxes. This shape helps them to dig tunnels through soft soil. Some types have large hind wings, which are folded under their short front wings. On warm evenings they often fly around slowly and noisily. Other types of mole crickets have short hind wings and cannot fly.

Mole crickets use their strong front legs to burrow into the ground.

Most mole crickets feed on roots, insects, and other creatures they come across in the soil. Because they live underground, people rarely see them but there are about fifty types, which live all over the world. The European mole cricket has been introduced into parts of North America and is often a pest in fields of root crops.

7
Watching and Listening

Bush crickets can be very difficult to find in the wild because many of them look like leaves.

Looking for grasshoppers and crickets can be fun. You can find the noisy ones by listening for their songs. Others are to be found by lifting up and looking under old boards or stones. Almost every meadow, roadside, or wooded area has its own special kinds of crickets and grasshoppers.

If you want to hear grasshoppers, choose a warm day and find a grassy place where you can sit quietly and listen to them singing. You can find adults by slowly creeping through the grass toward the sound.

Crickets are more difficult to find, because they are active mainly in the evening. The edges of woods and forests are good places to look for bush crickets. The large adults often sit on bushes in the warm sunshine of late afternoon. Later in the evening you can try to find them as they begin their evening chorus. Field crickets and mole crickets can often be found by quickly turning over boards or logs in grassy places where they live.

Crickets and grasshoppers make interesting pets. Most can be kept in a glass aquarium (without the water of course) covered by a net lid. In the aquarium you can place some soil, grass and other plants and a small log.

Most grasshoppers and crickets will eat plant leaves. Many will also eat lettuce and potato peelings. Try to find what else they like to eat. You must also include some drinking water.

An empty fish tank makes a good home for crickets and grasshoppers.

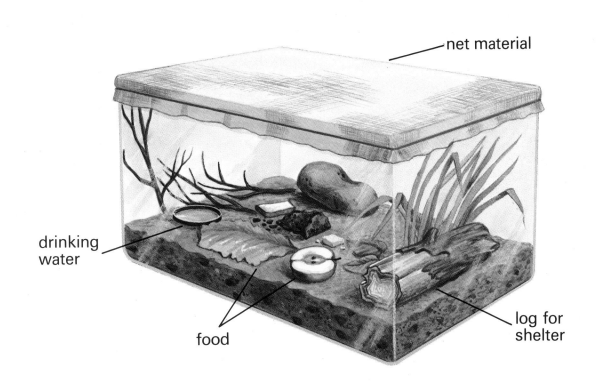

net material

drinking water

food

log for shelter

Glossary

Abdomen The rear part of an insect's body, containing the stomach.

Antennae The two feelers on the head of an insect, which are sensitive to touch and smell.

Camouflage The use of color, pattern or shape by which an animal's body matches its background and is therefore hidden.

Chitin The strong but light material that forms the "shell" of an insect and acts as both the skin and the skeleton.

Compound eyes The pair of large eyes found on many insects. Each compound eye is made up of many tiny lenses or facets.

Fungus A simple type of plant without green coloration, for example mushrooms and molds.

Hibernate To sleep through the winter.

Hoppers A special name given to the nymphs of locusts.

Larva The young stage of an insect and of some other animals.

Mandibles The sharp "teeth" of an insect's mouthparts.

Mating The joining together of a male and female animal to produce young.

Maxillae Parts of an insect's mouth that help to push in and chop up food.

Nymph The name for an insect larva that looks almost the same as the adult.

Ovipositor The part of a female insect's body that is used to lay eggs.

Palps Small feelers at the side of an insect's mouth, used for tasting food.

Parasites Small animals that live inside, or on, the body of another animal.

Pronymph A strange, legless type of larva, which hatches from the egg of a grasshopper or cricket. It lasts for only a minute or so before splitting open to reveal the tiny grasshopper or cricket.

Pupa The stage of some insects that comes between the larva and the adult.

Simple eyes Eyes made up of only one lens.

Sperm cells Cells produced by a male animal, which fertilize a female's eggs.

Stridulating Making a shrill sound, as a cricket does, by rubbing together certain parts of the body.

Thorax The middle part of an insect's body, bearing the legs and wings.

Finding Out More

If you would like to find out more about grasshoppers and crickets you could read the following books:

Boy Scouts of America. *Insect Life.* Irving, TX: Boy Scouts of America, 1973.

Cole, Joanna. *An Insect's Body.* New York: William Morrow, 1984.
Dallinger, Jane. *Grasshoppers.* Minneapolis, MN: Lerner Publications, 1981.
Darling, Kathy. *Ants Have Pets.* Easton, MD: Garrard, 1971.
Horton, Casey. *Insects.* New York: Franklin Watts, 1984.

Index

Picture Acknowledgments

All photographs from Oxford Scientific
Films by the following photographers:

T. Allen 19; G. I. Bernard 9, 17 (right), 21;
J. A. L. Cooke cover, frontispiece, 14, 20, 22, 30, 39, 41; S. Dalton 31; M. P. L. Fogden 32, 36, 42; B. P. Kent (Animals Animals) 40; Mantis Wildlife Films 37; S. Morris 35; P. O'Toole 27; K. Porter 8, 12, 38; D. Shale 26; P. Sharpe 11, 34; T. Shepherd 23; D. Thompson 13, 15, 24, 25, 28, 29; P. & W. Ward 33. Artwork by Wendy Meadway.